The Warrior Warring

Dear Pat:

Be brave (Judges 6:12)

Renée D. Warring
Saturday, 4/1/2017

The Warrior Warring

Renee D. Warring

Copyright © 2016 Renee D. Warring
All rights reserved.

ISBN: 0997096306
ISBN 13: 9780997096309

IF YOU ARE THINKING ABOUT COMMITING SUICIDE, OR YOU HAVE A PLAN ON HOW YOU WILL DO IT, PLEASE READ:

Help is close by. Visit www.suicide.org for suicide warning signs as well as a letter to people who are considering suicide. You can call 1-800-SUICIDE (1-800-784-2433) or 1-800-273-TALK (1-800-273-8255) 24 hours a day, seven days a week. These numbers can be called from anywhere in the United States. The second phone number gives you a listing of low-cost clinics in your area. If someone you know is in immediate danger, call 911 and stay with him or her until help arrives.

Never act on your thoughts or plans of committing suicide. Suicide is NEVER the answer. You cannot control the suicidal feelings by your own power. You need treatment through medication. You have a chemical imbalance in your brain; you cannot think straight. The imbalance can only be brought back into balance through medication.

If you are able, go to the emergency room or call 1-800-784-2433. Please make a commitment to staying alive! Do it for all of the people who care about you and love you. Do not cause pain in their lives; please think about them!

Suicide Warning Signs[1]

- Appearing depressed or sad most of the time (untreated depression is the number one cause for suicide)
- Talking or writing about death or suicide
- Withdrawing from family and friends
- Feeling hopeless
- Feeling helpless
- Feeling strong anger or rage
- Feeling trapped—like there is no way out of a situation
- Experiencing dramatic mood changes
- Abusing drugs or alcohol
- Exhibiting a change in personality
- Acting impulsively
- Losing interest in most activities
- Experiencing a change in sleeping habits
- Experiencing a change in eating habits
- Losing interest in most activities
- Performing poorly at work or in school
- Giving away prized possessions
- Writing a will
- Feeling excessive guilt or shame
- Acting recklessly

---

[1] Kevin Caruso, Executive Director of Suicide.org. Retrieved from http://www.suicide.org/suicide-warning-signs.html.

Suicide Prevention in Children and Youth

The information gathered here is from NAMI (National Alliance on Mental Illness).[2]

Do the following things to help a youth who is considering suicide:

- Remain calm
- Ask the youth directly if he or she is thinking about suicide
- Focus on your concern for his or her wellbeing and avoid being accusatory
- Listen
- Reassure the person that there is help and that he or she will not feel like this forever
- Do not be judgmental

---

[2] http://blog.nami.org/2015/01/suicide-prevention-can-we-talk.html
http://namisemn.org/resources/suicide-prevention/#prevention

- Provide constant supervision; do not leave the youth alone
- Remove means of self-harm
- Find help
- Do not keep suicidal thoughts secret; tell a parent, guardian, teacher, or school psychologist
- Parents, seek community mental health resources as soon as possible

IMPORTANT: Talking about suicide does not lead to it; it may save a life! Parents or guardians take on a critical role and must participate in the process.

Suicide Warning Signs For Children and Youth

- Prior suicide attempts
- Suicidal threats in the form of direct and indirect statements
- Suicide notes or plans
- Family history of suicides
- Making final arrangements (e.g., writing a will or giving away prized possessions)
- Preoccupation with death
- Recent violence
- Change in appearance or behavior (e.g., plummeting grades or productivity)
- Tearfulness
- Negativism
- Social isolation

Suicide Risk Factors

- Mental illness, including depression, conduct disorders, and substance abuse
- Family stress and/or dysfunction
- Environmental risks, including the presence of a firearm in the home
- Situational crisis (e.g., traumatic death of a loved one, physical or sexual abuse, or family violence)

Preface

It is my desire that this book would give hope to those who have mental illness, and enlighten those who do not have it.

Note: A Spanish version of this book will be coming soon. *Este libro será publicado en español muy pronto*

Acknowledgments

I thank my husband, Ellis Warring, for encouraging me to finish this book, which I have been working on since 2010. The book started as one subject and then went through a metamorphosis over the six-year period. I also thank my English teacher, Ms. Sandra Johnson, who watched me blossom into a creative writer over the years. She encouraged me to keep on writing. I would be remiss if I failed to thank my Senior Pastor Paul James, who has continually prayed for me these past 19 years during several psychiatric episodes. Thank you Pastor Randolph Walters, who saw some of my original writings six years ago and said that they showed great, God-given potential. I would also like to thank Anthony Spann, an author of many books himself, who edited some of my earlier works. A former pastor of my church, Pastor Albert C. Brown, exhorted me to "tell my story," after I became discouraged with the fear of being stigmatized in the public eye. I thank my state representative from Pennsylvania,

Margo L. Davidson, who let me interview her. She blessed me with her vast knowledge on the following topics that greatly affect people who have mental illness: the healthcare, law enforcement, and prison systems. Last, but in no way least, I wish to thank Nicole Rayfield who put in countless hours helping me with the detailed work of getting my book ready for publication. She designed the front cover of this book and helped me with the wording on the back cover.

Thank you everyone!
Renee D. Warring

Table of Contents

Suicide Prevention in
Children and Youth ix
Preface xiii
Acknowledgments xv
Mental Illness Definitions xix

Chapter 1	Horror of Horrors 1
Chapter 2	Head in the Clouds 3
Chapter 3	At the End of My Rope 6
Chapter 4	The Foreboding 8
Chapter 5	There Was Darkness 12
Chapter 6	Too Much Stress 19
Chapter 7	For Richer or Poorer, in Sickness and in Health 23
Chapter 8	The Stigma and Shame of Mental Illness 26
Chapter 9	The Clubhouse: My Road to Recovery ... 34
Chapter 10	The Healthcare System 40
Chapter 11	Politics 42
Chapter 12	Law Enforcement and the Prison System 46

Chapter 13	Spirituality That Leads to Recovery · · ·	48
Chapter 14	Man's Disabilities Are God's Abilities · ·	·55
Chapter 15	Two Poems from My Heart to Yours · · · ·	·57
	Conclusion ·	·61

DEFINITION OF MENTAL ILLNESS

"Mental illness is a condition in the brain that can severely affect a person's ability to perform the normal day-to-day activities of life. Mental illness is literally an illness of the brain. A biological change occurs in the brain of a person which disrupts and diminishes their thinking ability, mood, behavior, and overall normal functioning abilities."[3]

DEFINITION OF SCHIZOPHRENIA

"A psychotic disorder marked by severely impaired thinking, emotions, and behaviors. Schizophrenic patients are typically unable to filter sensory stimuli and may have enhanced perceptions of sounds, colors, and other features of their environment. They gradually withdraw from interactions with other people, and lose their ability to take care of personal needs and grooming."[4]

DEFINITION OF BIPOLAR DISORDER

"Formerly known as Manic Depression, is a mood disorder that causes radical emotional changes and mood swings from manic restless highs, to depressive listless lows. Most bipolar individuals experience alternating episodes of mania and depression."[5]

---

[3] www.thechallengesofmentalillness.com
[4] *The Free Dictionary by Farlex*
[5] Ibid.

DEFINITION OF SCHIZOAFFECTIVE DISORDER
"A mental illness that shares the psychotic symptoms of schizophrenia and the mood disturbances of depression of bipolar disorder. The symptoms are: hallucinations, delusions, thought and process disorder, and depression."[6]

---

6 Ibid.

One

Horror of Horrors

Malcolm and I stretch forth our hands toward heaven. Instantly, we take flight. We are gliding effortlessly through the air—higher, higher, and higher. We even go above the clouds! We are jubilant with laughter, light and carefree as we soar. This marvelous adventure goes on for quite some time. Then, almost as suddenly as our flight began, we make our landing. I look around wildly, but Malcolm is nowhere to be found! My heart panics. *Where has he gone?* I sense that something ominous is in the air. My heart is beating very rapidly now, and it is then I notice that I am invisible. I believe that no one can see me. However, I look around and suddenly there appears a crowd of menacing-looking boys and girls with clenched fists and grimaces on their faces! Somehow, even though I am invisible, they seem to have a sixth sense of exactly where I am. They begin to surround me in an ever-tightening circle. I am horrified as I realize they are about to assault me! Suddenly, I wake up in a cold sweat, finding myself in my bed. This horrible nightmare repeated itself during my elementary school years.

The horror of horrors.

Two

Head in the Clouds

"Renee, close your mouth!" my parents told me all the time. A few minutes later when the attention was off of me and it was quiet, pop!—my mouth would open unconsciously again. I was daydreaming. Honestly, I do not remember what I was daydreaming about, but my sense now is that I wanted to escape this cruel world. I wanted so desperately to be in a world filled with peace, love, and acceptance.

"Renee, what is the answer to five plus six?" asked the teacher.

Oh no, here I go again, I thought. *I have not been paying attention; I'm so embarrassed!* I gave her an answer, though I knew it wasn't correct.

To the best of my recollection, the daydreaming started when I was about five or six years old. For the most part, our home was a home of peace and love. My parents loved each other and they encouraged Malcolm, Camille, and me to love one another too. My parents loved us for our unique selves. Of course we had arguments, just like all families do, but we were a loving and affectionate family. So, what cruelty was I trying so desperately to escape? It was the cruelty of others outside of our home.

I am and always have been a sensitive, kindhearted person. Being sensitive, though, means that my feelings are easily hurt. As an adult, I have better control over my emotions. However, I still tend to be sensitive to harsh words and cruelty. As a child, it was very hard for me to hit another child back. I was convinced that if I hit my attacker back, I would get beat up. I knew that I was not a very good physical fighter by any stretch of the imagination! I would run, run, run all the way home just about every day.

Needless to say, I did not feel loved by the masses in elementary school. I didn't play with anyone during recess. I isolated myself in a corner of the fence that surrounded the schoolyard. I felt safe there. One day, a non-teaching assistant (NTA) coaxed me into playing a game of hopscotch with a group of girls. I very reluctantly played with them. While I was hopping on one foot, someone pushed me and I fell face down on the ground. My newly-grown two front teeth were badly chipped. I was screaming and crying hysterically with blood running down my face. I

The Warrior Warring

was horrified about what had just happened to me. As a result of this incident, I have a surgical pin in one of my front teeth. I also wear permanent porcelain caps over both of my front teeth.

Only twice during my entire elementary school years did I hit someone back. On one occasion, someone punched me in my sore arm where I had received a vaccination the day before. Suddenly, I found myself hitting the girl inside the classroom with a volley of punches. After the class went outside, her friend punched me in the stomach and knocked all the wind out of me. On the second occasion, I ran into the house after someone punched me. To my horror, my father demanded that I go back outside and "punch her in the nose." I was shaking, but I went outside and hit her; she proceeded to beat me up. In a strange twist of circumstances, we became the best of friends.

I do believe that my constant daydreaming was my attempt to escape from the bullying. As I reflect back, I realize that the daydreaming, isolation behaviors, and nightmares were the first signs of the onset of my mental illness.

Three

AT THE END OF MY ROPE

I eventually became fed up with the never-ending bullying and name-calling. Some kids called me "Weirdo" and "Holy Roller" (because my family and I spent a lot of time in church). Many called me "Phyllis Diller" (a famous comedian), because I was supposedly ugly like her, and because my last name was Dillard. One boy constantly called me "Contaminated," though I could never figure out why.

I was fed up with being threatened, afraid, beat up, and forced to run home from school. I devised a plan, saying to myself, "Why didn't I think of this earlier?" My brother Malcolm was big-boned, hefty, and could fight. I, on the other hand, was a tall, petite-boned featherweight who could not fight. He was just what I needed to solve my gigantic bully problem.

The Warrior Warring

I gave Malcolm my hit list and he proceeded to beat up kids after school for me. He also beat up two of the bullies right in the schoolyard during recess! Since Malcolm assaulted two kids during recess, the school psychologist was called. She tried to get him to answer questions about his seemingly indiscriminate assaulting of boys and girls, but he was loyal to me. Tight-lipped, he refused to answer any of her questions. The only answer he would offer was his famous one-liner: "I don't know." Realizing she was getting nowhere, she telephoned our father, who was home during the day because he worked at night. She asked if Malcolm was violent at home, to which our father responded, "No." When she told my dad what Malcolm did, he was just as puzzled as she was. They could not understand why Malcolm was displaying such violent behaviors all of a sudden. They were further puzzled when his belligerent behavior disappeared as suddenly as it had appeared. Malcolm and I did not divulge our secret to our father until after we became adults.

Four

THE FOREBODING

By the time I was in fifth grade at middle school, I was no longer being physically bullied, but I was still being teased. I continued to display learned isolation behaviors at recess, when I finally did come out for recess. I devised a new way of coping with the verbal abuse. I deliberately ate my lunch very slowly in the lunchroom so that I had to spend the least amount of time possible at recess. I still daydreamed during recess and sometimes in class.

Then, in the beginning of seventh grade, I suddenly awakened from my daydreams during class. In that moment, I made a conscious decision that I wanted to attend one of the top academic high schools in the city. I wanted to prove to everyone that I could get into and graduate from that school. Perhaps I felt this so strongly

The Warrior Warring

because I had been an underdog for so long. My grades up through sixth grade were average to slightly below average. I needed to excel in something—so why not academics?

It was then that my warrior quality began to manifest itself.

I boldly told my father and mother that I wanted to attend the Philadelphia High School for Girls (affectionately known as Girls' High). My father emphatically told me that I had to get my grades up to A's and B's. I saw this as a challenge, so I buckled down and studied with determination and perseverance. I became known as "the Bookworm."

Upon graduating from William T. Tilden Middle School, I was on the honor roll for my entire seventh and eighth grade years. Unfortunately, my first year of high school was spent at John Bartram High School, because I unknowingly missed the deadline for applying to the school of my choice. In tenth grade, I finally made it to Girls' High. This was very unfamiliar territory for me. For all of my educational life, I was accustomed to being in a "bell-shaped, normative curve" population. The population at my new school was atypical, skewed toward the genius end of the scale.

Academically, it was a very intense battle for me. I was nervous and uptight, like the "E" string on a violin. I studied with all my might. Still, I failed geometry in my first year and had to go to summer school, barely passing the class. You see, some of the fault lines in the foundation of my primary and secondary education levels were being exposed—such as how I struggled to pay attention in class when basic concepts were being taught.

Despite the cracks in my foundation, I passed the tenth grade! Eleventh grade ended and I failed English. I was off to summer school once again. This time though, something amazing happened; I earned an "A" in summer school! My instructor insisted that we write at least two paragraphs every day of the week. Soon after, he was so impressed by my writing that he called my parents about my unbelievable progress. My writing was filled with personal theology, philosophies, descriptions of beautiful things, and emotions. That summer, at the age of sixteen, I discovered that I could write creatively, and quite well! After that summer, however, I quit developing my writing talents. They lay dormant within me for decades, until my fifties when I felt a heavy burden on my heart to write about mental illness.

Academics weren't my only battle. In 1974, I represented the state of Pennsylvania in the semi-finals of the Progressive National Baptist Convention Oratorical Contest. It was held in Brooklyn, New York. I won the semi-finals, competing against Miss New York and Miss Washington D.C. This was a huge accomplishment for me! My father took a tape of my speech to one of the vice principals of Girls' High. Dr. Mary Wright was overjoyed by the content of my message, the crispness of my

The Warrior Warring

enunciation, and my enthusiastic and powerful delivery. She told my father that she now understood where I got my tenacity and power from—it was from God. Yet, she had a foreboding word for my father concerning me. She predicted that I would have a nervous breakdown because of the tremendous pressure I was under at Girls' High.

Against all odds, I graduated from Girls' High, on Friday, June 21, 1974. God had empowered me! The ceremony was held at the Academy of Music in Center City, Philadelphia. "*Vincit qui se vincit*" (Latin), or "He who conquers, conquers himself!" is the motto.

The warrior was warring!

Five

There Was Darkness

I enrolled in the Community College of Philadelphia after Girls' High. After two and a half years, I graduated with high honors and enrolled at Temple University. It was at Temple that I had the nervous breakdown Dr. Wright predicted. My diagnosis was schizophrenia. I was having visual and olfactory hallucinations (I believed that I was in hell and could smell wood burning). I felt hopeless because I believed that I committed the unforgiveable sin of blasphemy against the Holy Spirit in my thought life. The Pharisees, who were religious leaders in the Jewish religion, committed this sin. They saw Jesus' miracles, empowered by the Holy Spirit, and attributed them to the power of Satan. In later years, I learned that true followers of Christ cannot commit this unforgivable sin.

The Warrior Warring

I made four suicide attempts, one by cutting both wrists with surgical blades, and three by trying to overdose with sleeping pills. I could not go through with the suicide because I would remember how much my parents and siblings loved me. I would stop short of killing myself because I did not want to cause them any pain or deep sadness. I was experiencing mental and emotional pain and anguish, as well as spiritual warfare of the mind.

My parents took me to see a psychiatrist. I will not mention his name because he is deceased now. I will mention, however, that the type of psychiatry he practiced was orthomolecular psychiatry. This type of psychiatry believes that "mental diseases or abnormalities result from various chemical imbalances or deficiencies and can be cured by restoring proper levels of chemical substances, such as vitamins and minerals, in the body."[7] My psychiatrist put me on a diet in which I was not allowed to eat gluten, dairy, fungi (mushrooms and cheese), or yeast. The only grains I could eat were rice and corn. He wanted me to be in bed by 10:00 p.m. so that I could get seven to eight hours of sleep per night. I had to eat three meals a day on a consistent schedule, so as to cause my body as little stress as possible. He also said that I should have healthy snacks between meals. He wanted me to avoid high stress situations. Lastly, he prescribed vitamins and minerals. He believed in using the least amount and the lowest dosages possible of psychotropic medications.

---

7 *The American Heritage Stedman's Medical Dictionary*, 202

Please be clear that I am NOT prescribing the above-mentioned regimen for my readers. I am telling you what my doctor's treatment plan was for me. I believe in a more holistic approach to psychiatry. You will have to make up your own mind concerning your approach. As long as I adhered to my prescribed treatment plan, I was well and stayed out of psychiatric institutions. When I deviated from my treatment plan, I was eventually hospitalized.

Now that my psychiatrist is deceased, I have been searching for a new orthomolecular psychiatrist. I am realizing that here in Pennsylvania they are very hard to find and they do not accept insurance. I found one psychiatrist online who is willing to work out a payment plan with me, but I still cannot afford the payment plan.

Remember, we spend money on what is important to us, so be sure to use your money wisely. My philosophy concerning health is: Either you pay now or you will pay later, and it will be more costly later. Those of us who do not have enough income to afford such a doctor may seek someone who can help lessen the financial burden. As for me, I have not been able to find such a person.

I have been following the treatment plan of my deceased psychiatrist while seeing a traditional psychiatrist. I am proactive by knowing the side effects of my medications and getting a printout of the side effects from my pharmacist. If I experience side effects that affect my quality of life, I inform my psychiatrist right away and insist he change my medication or the dosage of it. Advocacy is important in this process. You can read about non-traditional treatments and see if your current psychiatrist will allow you to try them while still taking traditional medications. You may have to find an open-minded traditional psychiatrist. If you are comfortable and satisfied with your current treatment, then that is okay too.

I strongly believe that insurance companies must be more liberal and cover preventative, holistic, and alternative medical, psychiatric, and counseling practices. One example of a holistic practice is orthomolecular psychiatry. The determining factors in whether or not the insurance companies will cover a type of practice or treatment are the results of a double-blind study. "This type of study is a quantitative setup where neither the subjects nor the researchers know who has been assigned to the experimental group or the control (placebo) group until after the study is over. Double-blind construction ensures that the researchers do not skew the results by unintentionally affecting subject responses and/or outcomes."[8] "In addition, the results of the study would have to show a statistically significant improvement, over perhaps years, in the group that receives the treatment or participates in the procedure.

---

[8] Renee Grinnell, *Psych Central*, 2008

In a 2011 survey it was determined that out of 18 major HMOs and health insurers, 14 companies covered at least 11 or 34 alternative therapies. The ones that are most commonly covered are chiropractic care, acupuncture, and massage therapy. Most patients still must pay out of pocket for other complementary and alternative medicine (CAM) procedures and treatments."[9]

When I became ill during the time I attended Temple University, the doctor insisted that I withdraw from school and take time to heal using his treatment plan. I was very brokenhearted about this hope-crushing news. Deep within my heart, I had a very strong desire to finish school and get my bachelor's degree. I cried uncontrollably for a while, but I finally decided to withdraw from school, for what turned out to be one semester and the summer sessions.

Once again, the warrior mentality welled up in me. I was determined to get better so that I could go back and finish my degree. Finally, the doctor said that I had improved enough to resume my studies at Temple University; I was elated! In the back of my mind, I was still haunted by feelings of condemnation and guilt; somehow, I was able to ignore the thoughts and feelings because I knew that I had studying to do.

On May 29, 1980, the very thing I fought so vehemently for became a reality; against all odds, I walked

---

[9] "East Coast Health Insurance," *Health Insurance and Alternative Medicine*, 201

onto the stage at the commencement ceremony and received my bachelor of liberal arts degree with a major in psychology! I thank God so much for empowering me to accomplish this. It was amazing that my grade point average was a 2.99 in spite of what I had gone through!

Reflecting upon my bouts with mental illness, I have discovered that there are at least seven factors that play important roles in recovery from mental illness:

1. Having and maintaining a healthy and balanced brain chemistry though individualized treatments plans
2. Creating and maintaining a balanced and healthy psychological and emotional state through tailor-made therapies and counseling methods
3. Cultivating and maintaining healthy and vibrant family, caregiver, and advocate support systems that help and encourage us to become our optimum selves
4. Creating and accepting empathetic societal and community environments that cultivate our individual growth (e.g., clubhouses and community integration organizations)
5. Creating and maintaining economic and employment practices that encourage, support, and sustain us in finding and keeping the jobs

we desire, and empower us in our chosen business ventures
6. Becoming actively involved in the political and judicial systems by aiding government figures in the creation of bills, or supporting bills that fund and structure early intervention programs and individualized treatment programs (in order to prevent institutionalization)
7. Maintaining and nurturing an ongoing personal relationship with God

When discussing orthomolecular psychiatry, I focused on the brain chemistry aspect. Now I will focus on the psychological and emotional aspect of recovery.

I have been seeing a female Christian therapist since I won my disability case in 2007. The therapy has had a life-changing impact on my husband, our marriage, our son, and me. Under her therapy, I have been able to resolve some major issues, which could have resulted in life-altering catastrophes in my life. I urge people, especially those with a mental health diagnosis, to see a therapist regularly throughout their lifetime.

Six

Too Much Stress

My doctor included in my treatment plan for me to avoid high levels of stress. On November 30, 1980, I married the man I believed to be my knight in shining armor. It turned out to be a bad marriage. There was plenty of blame to go around, on my side as well as his. However, I will mention that the marriage, and subsequent divorce of 1982 were very stressful events that catapulted me into a deep depression. It was around this time that my diagnosis was more finely classified as bipolar disorder. I lost my job, went back to live with my parents, and applied for and received cash assistance—welfare. By God's grace, I successfully found and held a job as a Spanish teacher in a private high school in Philadelphia, while struggling with deep depression. At Temple, I had an undeclared minor in Spanish. To this day, I can speak, read, and write the language almost fluently.

I majored in psychology, which limited me to working with people, as opposed to working with things. I loved working with people, but the 20-plus years of grueling, high stress jobs took their toll on me. The road I took led me to numerous psychiatric episodes and nervous breakdowns. It was so bad that I regularly called in sick for several days just about every six months. Because of this, there were some gaps in my employment history. I was fired from at least two jobs. Throughout my employment history, I took three career paths: 1) Spanish teacher, 2) bilingual customer service representative, and 3) bilingual case manager. In one of the case management jobs, the goal was to preserve the families of abused and/or neglected children. In another case management job, I worked with the homebound senior citizen population to give them in-home services to improve their quality of life. I had a caseload of 120 people. It is an understatement that I experienced high levels of stress, which was the antithesis of what my doctor ordered.

I deeply pondered then, and still do now, where people like me with psychiatric diagnoses fit in the workforce. The vast majority of workplace settings were highly stressful, and are even more stressful today. There is a shrinking workforce and a heavier demand of work put on those that remain. I have clear memories of talk of the implementation of a four-day work week in the

The Warrior Warring

not-too-distant past. Now we are forced to work six or seven days, or at least longer hours during a five-day work week. I do not have the answer to resolve this serious, mentally unhealthy state of affairs. More people seem to exhibit mental health problems due to the extreme stressors of their jobs.

I reiterate, where do we (people with psychiatric diagnoses) fit in the workforce? Maybe we can be volunteers, but we have financial needs like everyone else! Perhaps we can hold down part-time jobs that are not too stressful, but this relegates us to poverty! Many of us are being herded into Certified Peer Specialist (CPS) positions, which can be a full-time, but not all of us possess the skillset or interest to be a CPS. A CPS is someone who works with people who have mental illness, as well as those who have mental illness in addition to drug and/or alcohol addictions. It is his or her job to instill hope, advocate for, empower, and help to improve the quality of life for the above-named population. CPS's generally have had similar life experiences as the people they are helping.

People with mental health diagnoses must have permanent accommodations in their jobs. The question is: What is the probability of this being strictly adhered to in a profit-driven society? "State vocational rehabilitation programs focus on pre-employment—where they train and place, rather than place and train. They focus on time-limited assistance, an approach that does not serve people with mental illness, whose need for support in the workplace may be long-term or intermittent. The price of this unmet need is exorbitant in human costs of wasted talent, derailed lives, broken families, lost productivity, and increased public spending on disability income and health care. People living with mental illness are the largest and fastest-growing group of public disability income beneficiaries."

The above-noted article also states, "Mental illness should no longer sentence people to poverty. People living with mental illness want to work, frequently can work and models have been developed to help them succeed. However, these effective interventions are few and far between. Multiple implementation barriers exist, including lack of political will, inadequate funding, misaligned policies, stigma, and discrimination against people with mental illness. Now is the time to leverage conversing trends to break the cycle of mental illness and serious commitment to implementing effective supported employment programs so that people with mental illness can recover and become contributing members of society."[10]

---

[10] "Road to Recovery: Employment and Mental Illness," 2014 by NAMI, National Alliance on Mental Illness

Seven

For Richer or Poorer, in Sickness and in Health

On March 29, 1987, I married my second husband, Ellis. I thank God for him. He really loves me. He has stood by me in sickness and in health, when most men would have left me. When I had psychiatric episodes just about every six months, he accompanied me to see my psychiatrist and nursed me back to health. We have been married for 28 years and are the proud parents of one son. I stand by his side as his helpmate. I love, strengthen, serve, and encourage him in his endeavors and interests.

It was very hard for the two of us to face the reality in 1998 that it was detrimental to my mental health for me to continue working. After all, we had a baby! With the emotional and spiritual support of our pastor, I resigned from my full-time job. Ellis stood by my side in this difficult decision.

Within a few months, I started working at a retail store part-time. I was able to work the hours that I requested for a while. However, within a short period of time, I was required to work at the behest of management. I could no longer work hours that worked around my responsibilities as a mother. It became more and more difficult for me to be home when my child needed me. In addition to this, I was required to work past 10:00 p.m., which was when my doctor told me to be in bed by. I presented a doctor's note to management. They were not consistent in honoring it, so I had no recourse but to resign. Soon, I got another part-time job. It was at this point that one of the elders of our church told us that my getting part-time jobs was not helping our household. She said that I needed to apply for Social Security Disability Insurance (SSDI) so that I could receive more income and not have to endure the stresses of holding down a job. We had to trust God to supply our needs while we waited to get SSDI. In other words, I had to completely stop working! This was a huge step of faith for us. Again, Ellis did not run from me, but stayed with our son and continued to work his full-time job. He did not pressure me to work, even though we applied for welfare and did not qualify because of his income. Ellis is a true man of faith.

The Warrior Warring

An elder from our church assured Ellis and me that we needed to trust God to provide for us. She also said that God would see to it that we would continue to have our house and our car. She served me by helping me through the entire process of getting my Social Security Disability Income (SSDI) benefit. She helped me to fill out the application and went to the Social Security Office with me to file for SSDI. She went with me to an appointment I had with a psychiatrist. He determined that I was not eligible for SSDI. Lastly, she was present at my hearing before a judge. I was finally given SSDI after a lengthy two-year process. I want to mention the fact that in the early 2000s, my mental health condition was more specifically identified as schizoaffective disorder.

I have been blessed by God to have the support of my husband, son, parents, siblings, mother-in-law, church family, and friends. These people in my life have been very instrumental in the nurturing and stabilizing of my mental health. If some of you do not have this kind of support, you may want to find and join a clubhouse in your area. A clubhouse is a supportive community for people with mental illness. You can make friends and meet empathetic staff. They can meet your needs for socialization, advocacy, nurturing, stabilization, and even employment. It is very important to have family, caregivers, and advocate support systems in place; they make the process of recovery sustainable.

Eight

THE STIGMA AND SHAME OF MENTAL ILLNESS

Some people do not value me. There are times that I wish I could be invisible. Many people who stigmatize those with a mental health diagnosis do not know why they do it. I believe the reasons are as follows: 1) It is a learned behavior that people acquire from their families; 2) some people have inferiority complexes and must posture themselves to be superior to someone else; and 3) people stigmatize out of ignorance and fear.

I tried to get a volunteer job in a non-profit organization. I wanted to do something simple, like filing. The director of the agency saw that I had some sort of condition because my hands trembled and I walked slowly. He

The Warrior Warring

asked me what my disability was and then proceeded to tell me why I could not work in his office. That was definitely discrimination!

From March 2008 to February 2009, I volunteered for food preparation at a rescue mission. I could certainly work—and quickly too! The food preparation team put food on 45–80 plates within 20 minutes. I must say that the director of the non-profit organization missed out on having an excellent and dedicated worker on his staff!

I found out through experience that many people who do not know me tend to treat me with disrespect when they find out that I have schizoaffective disorder. My mother told me not to tell anyone about my mental health diagnosis. She said, "When people find out that you have schizoaffective disorder, they will proceed to discriminate against you!" I found out that she was partially correct. What my mother did not realize was that there were (and are) many people who love me in spite of their knowledge of my disorder—including people in my church family and my long-standing female friends of 20-plus years. Although they love me, almost every one of those friends still underestimates the extent and magnitude of my talents and abilities, and tries to put me in a box. I am quite certain that God did not put me in a box, as some people do. I know for sure that I have God-given talents and abilities within me that people are not aware of! On the other hand, there are parts of me that even I am not aware of. All people are multifaceted! In 2008. one of the pastors of my church prophesied that I would be doing things that people had no clue that I could do. For example, I began praise dancing in my church at the age of 53 and I am still going strong at my present age of 59. I know that there are more great things to come!

Shame in My Game

Shame is born out of being stigmatized in many situations, or being a member of a family who taught shame. For me, it was the former. Each time I went to the counseling center, a big wave of shame would suddenly come over me. I did not want any of my coworkers or bosses to see me going inside of *that* building. I wished so intensely that there was a rear entrance. I did not want to lose my job because it was discovered that I was "crazy." Many people from my neighborhood went to that clinic for psychiatric treatment. I did not want people to see me there and discover that I had a psychiatric illness. Unfortunately, my worst fears were realized when a child recognized me from the school I worked in and told his mother my name and how he knew me. So much for confidentiality!

As a Christian, I meditate on two verses from the Bible to help me overcome shame. "I will praise You,

The Warrior Warring

for I am fearfully and wonderfully made; Marvelous are Your works, And that my soul knows very well" (Ps. 139:14, NKJV). And, "'For I know the plans I have for you,' declares the LORD, 'plans to prosper you and not to harm you, plans to give you hope and a future'" (Jer. 29:11, NIV).

When you see people with disabilities, DO NOT assume what their altitude will be in the Lord or what their altitude will be in life in general. God has power and he can rearrange people, things, and circumstances. As I yield myself to the Lord, he will determine my altitude in him and in life. As Christians, and as people in general, we must be careful not to write off people who have disabilities.

Where did stigma originate in the human race? How does stigmatization affect individuals internally and behaviorally, and who are its targets? How can we lessen the occurrences of stigmatization and discrimination against people with mental illness in society? Stigma had its origins in the Old Testament, specifically in Genesis 4:9–16. The stigmatized person was Cain, son of Adam and Eve, who was branded by God for killing his brother, Abel. Cain killed him because he was envious that God accepted Abel's sacrifice over his. The stigma was a mark, or *owtt* (pronounced "oat") in Hebrew. The *owtt* actually saved Cain's life. People knew that if they killed Cain, God would cause Cain's killer to suffer seven times more vengeance from God than Cain suffered.

Stigma can be defined as "archaic: a mark of shame or discredit."[11] In addition, it is "a set of negative and often unfair beliefs that a society or group of people have about something."[12] "The effects of stigma on people living with mental illness causes them to:

- Develop an intense fear of 'coming out';
- Delay seeking necessary mental health care;
- Develop a practice of self-stigmatization;
- Endure discrimination"

"The effect of stigma on people dealing with mental health issues is as painful as the mental disorders themselves. The stigma causes society to develop the following attitudes and actions toward people with mental illness:

- Fear;
- Mistrust;
- Prejudice;
- Violence against those with mental disorders."[13]

---

11 http://merriam-webster.com/
12 http://healthyplace.com/stigma/stand-up-for-mental-health/stigma-and-discrimination-the-effects-of-stigma
13 Ibid.

The Warrior Warring

"Frequently, stigma against people with mental health disorders involves propagation of inaccurate and negative perceptions—namely by the media. Movies and other media platforms often portray those with mental disorders as violent, incompetent, and disdainful. Perpetuation of hurtful and inaccurate stereotypes by the media is especially harmful because of the profound role it has in shaping and influencing social mores and attitudes. Whether consciously or not, the community as a whole ingests these negative attitudes, which they then use to stigmatize those with mental disorders."[14] Since the media is used as a tool to ingrain into the minds of society negative stereotypes about people with mental illness, it can also be used to erase those negative stereotypes. We who have mental illness have talents, abilities, aptitudes, and skills just as other people in our society do. Therefore, we must be allowed to use these qualities for the betterment of society. We must be given permanent opportunities to participate in society!

"Dr. Jeffery Swanson, a professor in psychiatry and behavioral sciences at the Duke University School of Medicine"[15] is one of the leading researchers on mental health and violence. Dr. Swanson stated, "We need to think of violence itself as a communicable disease. We have kids growing up exposed to terrible trauma.

---

14 http://propublica.org/article/myth-vs-fact-violence-and-mental-health
15 Ibid.

Renee D. Warring

We did a study some years ago, looking at [violence risk] among people with serious mental illness. The three risk factors we found were most important: first, a history of violent victimization early in life, second, substance abuse, and the third is exposure to violence in the environment around you. People who had none of those risk factors—even with bipolar disorder and schizophrenia—had very low rates of violent behavior."[16] "If someone has a history of any kind of violent or assaultive behavior, that's actually a better predictor of future violence than having a mental health diagnosis."[17]

"The vast majority of people with mental illnesses are not violent. Although studies suggest a link between mental illnesses and violence, the contribution of people with mental illnesses to overall rates of violence is small, and further, the magnitude of the relationship is greatly exaggerated in the minds of the general population (Institute of Medicine, 2006)."[18] "People with psychiatric disabilities are far more likely to be victims than perpetrators of violent crime (Appleby et al., 2001)."[19] "People with severe mental illnesses, schizophrenia,

---

16 Ibid.
17 http://depts.washington.edu/mhreport/facts-violence.php
18 Institute of Medicine, *Improving the Quality of Health Care for Mental and Substance-Use-Conditions.* Washington D.C.: Institute of Medicine, 2006.
19 Appleby, L., Mortensen, P. B., Dunn, G., & Hiroeh, U. (2001). Death by homicide, Suicide, and other unnatural causes in people with mental illness: a population-based study. *The Lancet,* 358, 2110-2112.

bipolar disorder or psychosis are 2 ½ times more likely to be attacked, raped or mugged than the general population (Hiday, et al., 1999)."[20]

---

20 Hiday, V. A., Swartz, Swanson, J. W., et al. (1999). Criminal victimization of persons with severe mental illness. *Psychiatric Services*, 50, 62-68.

Nine

THE CLUBHOUSE: MY ROAD TO RECOVERY

In 2007, I had been waiting for two years for my Social Security Disability hearing to be scheduled. I grew tired of the waiting. If it were not for the fact that my husband was working, we would be on welfare by now, living with family or friends, having lost the house, or living on the streets.

Unexpectedly, I was notified of a hearing date via the mail. I attended the hearing and ended up winning the case. Thank God! Feeling euphoric, and on an emotional high, I told myself, *I've got money—lots and lots of money!*

The lump sum cash payment quickly ran out and reality suddenly set in. Was I going to spend the rest of my life looking forward to collecting a monthly check? Was

The Warrior Warring

I going to sit here and knit baby booties for the rest of my life? I felt like I had one foot in the grave and one foot on a banana peel! I was dying inside—devoid of hope, aspirations, and vision. Worst of all, I was afraid to do anything productive, for fear that the Social Security Administration would take away my benefits that I so vehemently fought for!

Many of my family and friends saw me as hopelessly sick. According to them, I would always be this way, but my intuition told me otherwise. I knew that I had talents, gifts, abilities, and skills that were not being utilized. This was a seed of hope!

I adjusted my attitude and belief in God and myself. I knew there were others in my family who believed in me: my sister, my parents, and my maternal aunt—all of whom made me feel valuable and saw me as being well. My sister reminded me of how in years past, I was full of life and energy. These family members were cultivating seeds of hope and self-confidence in me that would lead to my doing enjoyable things again!

I took steps toward self-advocacy and spoke with my therapist, telling her what was going on in my mind and with my emotions. She encouraged me to get involved with a community of my peers at the Welcome House Clubhouse, located in Upper Darby, Pennsylvania. I became a member in November of 2008. The Welcome House Clubhouse is a community consisting of non-judgmental, supportive, and loving staff and members. I was encouraged to make my own goals, be courageous, and to hope again! One of my goals was to write articles for the Welcome House Clubhouse newsletter, *Echoes of Welcome*. In time, I did. I was later invited to join the committee for Elwyn in Pennsylvania for the publication of the *CARE Newsletter*.

In addition to writing, I succeeded in horticulture. I took care of plants in the Welcome House greenhouse. I soon realized that growing and caring for plants exemplifies a process of self-renewal. During this time, I decided that I wanted to become a CPS (Certified Peer Specialist). I enjoyed encouraging, empathizing with, and advocating for people with mental illness. I became a CPS in June of 2009 and continue to volunteer one day a week at New Visions, in Philadelphia, Pennsylvania (a part of Elwyn).

I am elated by the fact that people like me with mental illness can set goals, regain hope, and even recover from mental illness. I am in a deep emotional process, but I am more than glad to have my "groove" back—an even bigger and better groove now!

Joining the Welcome House Clubhouse was the best decision that I made. Not only did the activities keep me occupied in a positive way, but the staff and members helped me regain self-confidence in my writing and public speaking abilities. I also became proficient in

The Warrior Warring

using the computer. Many days at the Welcome House were just plain fun! One year at a talent show, I performed a solo dance skit. I did my skit to the song "I'm Coming Out" by Diana Ross. In the skit, I made my way out from amongst the audience. I was hunched over like an old lady, walking with a cane. Upon reaching the stage, I dropped my coat, which I had draped over my shoulders (James Brown style), put on my sunglasses, and put on my red Kangol cap with the brim tilted to one side. I threw away my cane and began to dance vigorously. I won second place in the dance contest! At the holiday party in December of 2013—at the age of 56—I won first place in the dance contest, competing against all young people, to which the audience was amazed and I was very elated! I have already decided that I will not compete if there is a dance contest at the 2014 holiday party; I will let the young people have a chance to win.

At another holiday party, I sang "Feliz Navidad" a cappella. The audience had no idea that I could sing! Later that year, I gave a speech entitled, "Stigma and Mental Illness." After my presentation, I sang "The Impossible Dream," from the play *The Man from La Mancha* (or should I say, *The Woman from La Mancha*?). I sang all the words from memory, a cappella, on key, and with great conviction. The audience was spellbound and some even cried.

Renee D. Warring

You may be asking yourself, "What is a Clubhouse?" Before I answer that question, I want to state what Clubhouse International's vision is for me and other people with mental illness. "Our vision is that there will one day be Clubhouses in the cities and towns of every country in the world."[21] "A Clubhouse is first and foremost a local community center that offers people who have mental illness hope and opportunities to achieve their full potential..."[22] "A Clubhouse is most importantly a community of people who are working together to achieve a common goal..."[23] "During the course of their participation in a clubhouse, members gain access to opportunities to rejoin the worlds of friendships, family, employment and education and to the services and support they may individually need to continue their recovery."[24] "A Clubhouse provides a restorative environment ..."[25] where people like me, who have mental illness, can receive support. We know that mental illness is not a death sentence; it is treatable and we can and do recover from it![26]

"The first Clubhouse was founded in New York City in 1948. It was later named Fountain House. The founders were comprised of a small group of people

---

21 http://www.iccd.org/whatis.html
22 http://iccd.org/mission.html
23 http://iccd.org/whatis.html
24 Ibid.
25 Ibid.
26 Ibid.

who had been recently discharged from a state psychiatric hospital, and who had decided to create a group they named, 'We Are Not Alone' or WANA. The building which they named Fountain House was purchased in 1950."[27]

---

[27] http://iccd.org/history.html

Ten[28]

The Healthcare System

Our healthcare system for people with mental illness leaves a lot to be desired. We who have mental illness have a brain disorder, or a chemical imbalance of the brain. We do not *cause* the condition—it happens *to* us! Our nation should regard those with mental illness, not only those with physical disorders. Our being put in a mental hospital is not treatment; it merely stabilizes us. We are heavily medicated to ensure that we are not a threat to others or ourselves. Upon discharge from the mental institution, we are given a prescription for lower dosage(s) of medication(s) and a promise that we will receive treatment from a psychiatrist within 72 hours after being discharged—which never materializes for most of

---

[28] Chapter Ten: Interview with PA. State Representative Margo Davidson of the 164th Legislative District, on Friday, September 12, 2014.

us. In many instances, patients are on a waiting list that extends from one to three months after hospitalization. When they are finally able to get an appointment with a psychiatrist, their encounter with the doctor usually lasts for only fifteen minutes!

Research tends to show that treatment works if the person is put into an individualized life treatment plan. As a result, he or she can emerge from the disease as a productive, contributing member of society. A tremendous breakdown of our society is a lack of timely, adequate, and individualized treatment. There should be comprehensive wellness communities developed where people feel good about themselves and can receive individualized treatment. Within the wellness community, the person's individual strengths can be identified and leveraged so that the person can be successful, and their weaknesses can be supported and their triggers minimized. With this model of treatment, the person can live a productive life.

The number one cause of death among people with mental illness is suicide. Many people who have mental illness do not seek out treatment for fear of being stigmatized by society. We are losing people in large numbers to suicide—people who could have contributed their talents, abilities, and gifts to our communities and to our nation.

Eleven

POLITICS

Many of us are not knowledgeable or informed—and much less participate—in the political system of our city, town, state, or country. Each of us must have a voice in our political system! None of us can complain about our government unless we are first registered to vote, and then actually do vote in a well-informed manner. If we are not part of the solution, we are part of the problem!

I registered to vote at the age of 18 and I am now 59. I have only missed voting in one election due to illness. Having a voice in our government is extremely crucial because if we do not have a voice, powerful lobbyists or other people who do not have our best interest at heart will determine our overall quality of life, or lack thereof. I am an active participant in a grassroots lobbying group in Pennsylvania called "Take Five" (meaning, take five

The Warrior Warring

minutes). The group is made up of people who have mental illness and caregivers of people who have mental illness. We call, email, and write those in political power to persuade them to vote on bills in a way that benefits us. I have traveled on a bus with the group to Harrisburg, Pennsylvania, and have physically gone to the offices of senators and state representatives to make our presence felt and our views known. We must all be proactive and not reactive. Complaining about our "lot" in life will get us nowhere. We are victors, not victims!

I was born in the 1950s, during the beginning of the civil rights movement, and I learned a lot by living in that era. I have a very important point to prove about the civil rights of people in general, not just the civil rights of people who have mental illness. The Emancipation Proclamation was signed by President Abraham Lincoln on January 1, 1863. It states: "And by virtue of the power, and for the purpose aforesaid, I do order and declare that all persons held as slaves within said designated States, and parts of States, are and henceforward shall be free."[29] My question to you is: Did this new law make the African American people free as intended? The answer to this question is a resounding "NO." After the Civil War was over in 1865, African Americans, who fought in the Civil War, were promised that they would gain freedom and civil rights equal to the other citizens of America. However, they were once again denied their civil rights.

---

29 http://historynet.com/emancipation-proclamation-text

Instead, Reconstruction came, which was followed by the enactment of Jim Crow Laws. In other words, the southern states were allowed to pass and enforce segregation laws. The fight for racial equality dragged on!

On July 2, 1964, then-President Lyndon B. Johnson passed the Civil Rights Act of 1964, which outlawed discrimination based on "race, color, religion, or national origin."[30] The backbone of this law was based on the Fourteenth and Fifteenth Amendments to the Constitution of the United States of America. Once again, I ask the question: Were the African American people set TOTALLY free as a result of the passage of the Civil Rights Act of 1964? I do admit that we were given more freedom than we had before, but we were not totally set free. Therefore, because discrimination still existed, the passage of the Voting Rights Act of 1965 was necessary. This law was also based on the Fourteenth and Fifteenth Amendments to the Constitution. It prohibited racial discrimination in voting.[31] President Johnson signed this law also. Although I have been focusing on the fight for the civil rights of African American people, I am making a broader point concerning us who have mental illness. The point is, we will NEVER get to the place where we as a people can rest and think that we have it made. We

---

30 http://ourdocuments.gov/doc.php?=flash=true&doc=97&page=transcript

31 http://ourdocuments.gov/doc.php?flash=true&doc=100page=transcript

The Warrior Warring

must continue to fight for our rights, generation after generation! The moment that we become comfortable, rest, and stop fighting, the advances we made will be turned back or made null and void.

Twelve[32]

LAW ENFORCEMENT AND THE PRISON SYSTEM

I interviewed Margo L. Davidson, a state representative, regarding law enforcement and the prison system. She made a point that many times, law enforcement has to make quick decisions when someone is breaking the law or being a threat to others. They do not have time to determine if the person is having a mental health episode or if he or she is a criminal. After the person is arrested, there must be a routine assessment system in place to determine this.

State Representative Davidson stated that many people in prison have mental illness. Our prisons have become mental institutions, as Sister Mary Scullion of

---

[32] Chapter Twelve: Interview with PA State Representative Margo Davidson, Friday, September, 12, 2014

The Warrior Warring

Project HOME in Philadelphia predicted two decades ago. There is a grave lack of mental health treatment available in our prisons today. There might be one or two psychiatrists assigned to thousands of prisoners. The prison system needs to have procedures in place to identify prisoners who are criminals and those who have mental illness. Adequate psychiatrists and mental health personnel must be hired and trained to identify and treat people who have mental illness. These people must be put in treatment environments, not in prison! State Representative Davidson has developed parts of legislation that will address these things. People are unique in their genetic makeup, skills, abilities, temperaments, personalities, beliefs, and so on. Therefore, the comprehensive treatments should address each person's individuality.

Thirteen

SPIRITUALITY THAT LEADS TO RECOVERY

Within democracy, we can practice any religion we want, or none at all. I put my faith in the finished work of Christ. I am a follower of Jesus Christ and this has made all the difference for me in this world and in my eternal life. At the age of eight, I entrusted my life to the Lord. I remember the day it happened. I did something wrong (now I can't remember what) and my dad spanked me. He did not abuse me by breaking my skin, bones, or injuring me in any way. Instead, he gave me a spanking and left me in the room alone to think about it. It was then that I realized the truth about myself: I was a sinner who needed Jesus. So, I knelt down on the side of the bed and prayed to receive Christ. Suddenly, a joy came over me! I ran downstairs to tell my family that Jesus came

The Warrior Warring

into my heart. They all rejoiced with me! The very next day I was so overjoyed that I made an announcement to the class of my encounter with Jesus. I raised my hand, the teacher called on me, I rose to my feet and made a clear announcement that I received Christ as my personal Savior the night before, and then I sat down. There was an eerie silence and stares from everyone, including the teacher! I could not understand why my classmates were not filled with joy for my decision, just as my family had been the night before. It was then that the bullying began.

Miracles of March–November 2013

At some point, I stopped following the treatment regimen that my former psychiatrist gave me. It was during that time that I experienced three psychiatric hospitalizations. In 2011, I began to once again follow the entire regimen, after taking stock of my condition. Due to limited finances, I began seeing a psychiatrist who is not an orthomolecular psychiatrist. My former doctor passed away around that time. However, I began to follow the regimen on my own accord, even though I was seeing a regular psychiatrist. In March of 2013, I was taken completely off of haloperidol (Haldol), a powerful anti-psychotic medication. I was experiencing incontinence of the bowel and bladder, which is one of the possible side effects of the medication. This was very hard on me because it was so embarrassing. These things seemed to always happen to me when I was out in public. I confronted my psychiatrist and told him exactly what was going on, showed him the list of side effects, and told him emphatically that I was not going to wear diapers at my young age! He took me seriously and told me that I no longer had to take the medication. To this day, I am not experiencing any psychosis.

In May of 2013, I was taking 30 mg of aripiprazole (Abilify) per day. I was experiencing severe leg cramps that were so painful that I could not stand. Once again, I showed my doctor the severe side effects that I was having and he took me off of it in increments. One month later, I was completely off of aripiprazole. To this very day, my psychiatrist has seen no need to put me back on these drugs. He put me on a low dosage of risperidone (Risperdal) per day. He also cut my clonazepam (Klonopin intake in half. He has been watching me very closely for over a year, and my medication intake remains in its reduced state. In addition, the dosage of lithium carbonate that I have to take is "below therapeutic levels." Both my psychiatrist and my therapist have declared that God has healed me! I inquired of them, "Why I must still take medications since God has healed me?" They said that it is because the medications I am

The Warrior Warring

taking are helping my brain chemistry to stay balanced and healthy.

I stated earlier that I struggled with feelings and thoughts of condemnation from the age of 21 until the age of 57. I believed that I committed the unforgiveable sin of blasphemy against the Holy Spirit. As time went on, I also developed the fear that I worshipped Satan in my thought life. This was very frightening for me! Those feelings, thoughts, and beliefs surfaced whenever I experienced high stress levels on the job and in life situations (divorce, marital problems, family problems, etc.). They would manifest through sleep deprivation, which only intensified the problem. They also surfaced when I failed to adhere to the regimen my former psychiatrist gave me.

The Bible says that Satan accuses us before God, but to no avail. In November of 2013, 2 Corinthians 10:5 jumped out at me from the pages of the Bible: "We demolish arguments and every pretension that sets itself up against the knowledge of God, and take captive every thought to make it obedient to Christ" (NIV). Suddenly, the meaning and application of this verse came alive to me and became a part of me. I must tear down and discard untrue thoughts and beliefs and replace them with the Word of God. It is true that my thought life was affected by chemical imbalances; however, as a believer in Christ I have and will experience battles of the mind. The first step I had to take to quiet my mind was to get the brain chemistry balanced through treatment. The second thing I had to do was put on the full armor of God (Eph. 6:10–18). I must subject EVERY thought to Christ.

In November, the Lord led me to recite and insert my name into Romans 8:1–2. I used the New International Version (NIV) of the Bible. I said, "Therefore, there is now no condemnation for me, Renee Warring, who is in Christ Jesus, because through Christ Jesus the law of the Spirit of life set me free from the law of sin and death." As I repeated the verse with conviction, suddenly the Holy Spirit manifested himself as a stream of air that rushed into my nostrils, down into my gut, and up to the front of my brain. I felt a weight lift off my head as the Holy Spirit streamed back and forth to the front and back of my head. Now I walk with my head held high, instead of having my head bowed and my neck bent down as it was in the past.

The Holy Spirit led me to declare Romans 8:38–39, "For I am convinced that neither death nor life, neither angels nor demons, neither the present nor the future, nor any power, neither height nor depth, nor anything else in all creation will be able to separate me from the love of God that is in Christ Jesus my Lord" (NIV). Through believing God's Word, Satan's deceptions were broken. The Holy Spirit set me FREE! The

The Warrior Warring

Lord knew that Satan would try to put me back into bondage by having me feel guilty about the "wasted" 36 years of my life being bound to his lies. If he was successful in doing this, he would have hampered me from effectively serving the Lord, due to guilt. Immediately, Romans 8:28 came to my mind, "And I know that in all things God works for the good of [Renee] who loves him, who has been called according to his purpose" (NIV). I went through what I did so I could be a help others; hence, this book!

A few days later, the Holy Spirit poured Revelation 5:13b into my mind, "Blessing and honor, glory, and power, be unto Him who sits upon the throne and unto the Lamb forever and ever!" (KJV). I repeated that verse in a loud voice of deep worship to God. Suddenly, there was great power in my voice; my voice became richer, fuller, and my chest and diaphragm resonated with authority and great power! When I realized I was changing, I became fearful. Immediately, 2 Timothy 1:7 came to my mind, "God has not given us the spirit of fear, but a spirit of power, of love and a sound mind" (KJV). I took heart and continued to worship. Immediately after I worshipped the Lord, the Holy Spirit led me to declare in a loud, powerful voice with great authority, Philippians 2:10a–11, " . . . that at the name of Jesus every knee shall bow, and every tongue confess that Jesus Christ is Lord, to the glory of God the Father" (KJV). I want to make it very clear that in NO WAY have I arrived spiritually! I am just a sinner saved by the grace of God. I have much more spiritual growing to do until the day I die.

Fourteen

Man's Disabilities Are God's Abilities

"You shall know the truth and the truth shall make you free" (John 8:32, KJV). What man labels as a "disability" is God's ability and opportunity. Why do we call it a "disability" anyway? The Lord looked on what he made and said that it was "very good" (see Gen. 1:26–31). Could it be that our mindsets and hearts are not pure? Could it be that the concept of "disability" in the human heart is a means of discriminating, oppressing, and dehumanizing what God has called "very good"? "But who are you, O man to talk back to God? Shall what is formed say to him who formed it, 'Why did you make me like this?' Does not the potter have the right to make out of the same lump of clay some pottery for noble purposes and some for common use?" (Rom. 9:20–21, NIV)

It is true that sin entered the world through Adam, marring creation and bringing pain, suffering, disease, death, and so forth. Nevertheless, we are all still made in the image of God (Gen. 1:26). Remember, what we call a "disability" is God's ability or tool to transform us. The Apostle Paul's "thorn in the flesh" (2 Cor. 12:7) became God's tool to humble him. God wants to get glory from our lives any way he can! Through the "thorn in our flesh"—for example, our mental illness—God keeps us humble so that we will not become proud and think that we are self-sufficient. It is God's reminder to us that we always need him. God can use our mental illness to remind us to give grace and be forgiving, loving, and helpful toward others. Lastly, God causes us to become a testimony that gives others with mental illness hope that God can do miraculous works through them too. It is through us, his clay, that his glory shines (Romans 9:20-21, NIV).

Fifteen

Two Poems from My Heart to Yours
By Renee D. Warring

"Grace"
(Isaiah 64:6; Ephesians 2:8–9)

Narrator:	Judgment we all deserve!
Person:	S'cuse me—you've got your nerve!
	For I'm a real good guy;
	I'm going to the sky!
Narrator:	But have you ever lied?
	Or lusted with your eyes?
Person:	Oh, those are little sins!
	I still will make it in;
	My good outweighs my bad.
Narrator:	Tell me what scales you've had?
	Have you been keeping track?
	Each thought, each word, each act?

Renee D. Warring

> Can you really be sure,
> You'll make it through that door?

"Hope"
(Isaiah 64:6; Romans 3:23; Romans 6:23; Romans 5:8; 1 John 2:2; 1 Corinthians 15:3; John 14:6; Romans 10:9–10; Hebrews 10:25)

God my maker has no sin,
Will I ever make it in?
    Nothing satisfies anymore.
    What has life for me in store?
Tried it all; it makes no sense,
What do I live for from hence?
    Emptiness is in my heart,
    Wish to make a brand new start!
Help someone, please help me, please!
I want help; I'm on my knees!
    "I will wash you white as snow."
    Who said that, I want to know?
I am Jesus Christ the Lord,
I will give you life restored!
    I will give your life meaning,
    Fill the void, a new being!
All your heart give it to me,
Tell me, I your master be!

The Warrior Warring

Prayer
I have sinned before you God,
Wash me in Christ Jesus' blood.
Jesus Christ my Master be!
Now, I know I'll make it in!
He has washed me of my sin!

Conclusion

I trust that from reading this book, those who do not have mental illness have received more insight into the internal struggles and pain of those of who do. I also trust that readers have become more empathetic toward those with mental illness, and perhaps more willing to begin to include them in the mainstream of society.

In summary, the steps that I, and many others, have used to recover from mental illness include:

1. Having and maintaining a healthy and balanced brain chemistry though individualized treatments plans;
2. Creating and maintaining a balanced and healthy psychological and emotional state through tailor-made therapies and counseling methods;
3. Cultivating and maintaining healthy and vibrant family, caregiver, and advocate support systems that help and encourage us to become our optimum selves;

4. Creating and accepting empathetic and fertile societal and community environments that cultivate our individual growth (e.g., clubhouses and community integration organizations);
5. Creating and maintaining economic and employment practices that support us in finding and keeping the jobs we desire, and empower us in our chosen business ventures;
6. Becoming actively involved in the political and judicial systems by aiding government figures in the creation of bills, or supporting bills that fund and structure early intervention programs and individualized treatment programs, to prevent institutionalization; and
7. Maintaining and nurturing an ongoing personal relationship with God.

I am overjoyed to have discovered that my major contribution to this world is writing and speaking on behalf of people who have mental illness. I have finally found my niche! Through my pain and suffering, I have been strategically positioned by God to serve others!

My name, "Renee," is a French name which means *warrior* and *reborn*. Both descriptions are true about me (I am definitely reborn in Christ); however, it is the first meaning that I am highlighting in this book. I truly believe that the Holy Spirit prompted my parents to name

The Warrior Warring

me Renee. My parents have often told me how they wanted to name me Valerie Denise Dillard. Somehow, the two of them had no inner peace about that name. They had no idea at the time what God's plan was for my life. Throughout this book, you have seen that I have been and am a warrior. Not only do I champion the cause of others who have mental illness, I am also a warrior advancing the Kingdom of God. My spiritual callings are to be an intercessory prayer warrior, evangelist, exhorter, teacher, and enactor of mercy and kindness for others. It is also no accident that I married a man named Ellis Warring. Thus, this book is appropriately titled, *The Warrior Warring*.

I would like all of my readers to read and put into practice a book entitled *The Bondage Breaker*, by Neil T. Anderson.[33] This book played a significant role in my spiritual healing. It is about overcoming negative thoughts, irrational feelings, and habitual sins. Please be very mindful that those of us who have chemical imbalances in our brains must first address those before we do anything else. Another book by the same author, *Victory Over the Darkness Study Guide*, is a companion to the first.[34] Please also read this book and put it into practice.[35]

---

[33] Copyright 2000. Published by Harvest House Publishers Eugene, Oregon 97402 ISBN 0-7369- 0241-4.

[34] ISBN 978-764213672

[35] Neil Anderson's books are already available in Spanish. (Los dos libros de Neil Anderson he sido publicado en español.)

Renee D. Warring

From October 2011 to June 2014, I greatly struggled within myself about writing and publishing this book. I had a strong desire to write this book because I knew it would set people free from bondages on many levels. I was going to publish using a pen name because I feared the loss of my projected persona as a "normal" member of society. In short, I wanted to avoid being stigmatized in the public eye. I was faced with the reality that since September 11, all information is now public domain. Even if I were to copyright my work under a pen name, my given name would eventually be revealed. I realized that it was God's will to publicly identify me.

In the summer of 2014, one of the former pastors of my church, Pastor Albert C. Brown from CareView Community Church, challenged me by saying: "You must tell your story!" I knew that it was the Lord speaking to me. Since that day, I have never looked back. I started writing until the book was finished.

Many people knew of the planned writing and publishing of this book years ago. Before I could write it, I needed to be transformed as a person. The focus of this book had to go through a metamorphosis as well. The original idea for the structure of this book was for it to be a collection of stories on the lives of many people who have mental illness, to prove that we are valuable to society. However, that was not the way the Lord wanted it to be written. John 12:24-25 (NIV) in The Holy Bible states: "Very, truly I tell you, unless a kernel of wheat falls to the

The Warrior Warring

ground and dies it remains only a single seed. But if it dies it produces many seeds. Anyone who loves their life will lose it, while anyone who hates their life in this world will keep it for eternal life." I was the one chosen to be the kernel of wheat that had to die. I had to die to my projected persona and be transparent before the eyes of the whole world. It was a must for me to do this, so that other people can live meaningful and fulfilled lives.

All glory to God! God bless you all! Amen.

Made in the USA
Middletown, DE
26 December 2016